1000 COOKING

SUBSTITUTIONS

1000 COOKING SUBSTITUTIONS

BY DEBBIE KHOEE

GLOBAL TRADE CO., INC.
BETHANY, OK 73008

Published by Global Trade Co.
P.O. Box 571
Bethany, OK 73008

First Edition
First Printing

LIBRARY OF CONGRESS
CATALOGING IN PUBLICATION DATA

Khoee, Debra Ann , 1954
1000 Cooking Substitutions
p. cm.
Includes Index
1. Food - Dictionaries   I. Title
TX357.K45   641.5   LC# 89-083816
ISBN# 0-9622451-8-6 (Hardcover)
ISBN# 0-9622451-7-8 (Softcover)

DEDICATION

This book is dedicated to all those who had to drive to the grocery store to finish dinner.

TABLE OF CONTENTS

NOTE TO READER

All the substitutions are listed directly underneath the ingredient you need which has been capitalized. They are not necessarily interchangeable. For instance, you may want to substitute peanut oil if olive oil is called for, but you may not necessarily want to substitute olive oil for peanut oil. Often many choices are given for a particular ingredient. It is left to the reader to choose the most suitable substitution.

The most frequently used measurements are given for your convenience. For instance, 1 tablespoon of cornstarch rather than 1 cup, would be listed.

This book was written by consulting every available cookbook in the metropolitan library system, as well as private collections. The most common substitutions found have been listed here. When there was a difference of opinion, an average was taken. For instance, if one book said to use 1 1/3 cups of a certain ingredient, and another book said to use 1 2/3 cups, then 1 1/2 cups was listed. Because of these differences of opinion, this book should be used as a general guide only.

It should be noted here that any given substitution may or may not present itself as an exact replacement of the original ingredient. What tastes fine in one dish may taste different in another. Because each person has different personal tastes, it is better to be conservative and assume that a substitution will alter the taste of the product, even though it may not alter it at all. Only through experimentation can you decide which of the substitutions available work best for you. Testing a small amount first is the best way to know for sure in advance whether or not you like the combination.

Another important point is that if you were brought up on a particular taste, such as real butter for instance, it would probably be best not to substitute for that ingredient at all.

Every effort was made to obtain the best available substitutions, and to eliminate obvious substitutions that need not be mentioned. We continually strive to collect more substitutions. There are actually over 1200 substitutions in this book. If you can help us with a substitution you know, please do. We want all the good substitutions we can find so that we can continually expand the collection, and with it the choices available.

Although a substitution can not be found for everything, and although a given substitution may not be appropriate in all circumstances, it is my sincere hope that a suitable substitution can be found in this book for what you need, and that it will save you a trip to the grocery store.

BREAD & BREAD CRUMBS

For those times when you want meatloaf or meatballs, but have no bread crumbs, shredded potatoes make good substitutes.

Many times you may want to coat something but need a substitute for bread crumbs or flour. You can use rolled oats, cornflakes, wheat germ, cracker crumbs, or perhaps cornmeal. More unusual substitutes would be matza meal, semolina grain meal, or sunflower seed meal which gives a nutty taste. The choice is up to you, of course.

BISCUITS

1 = 1 buttermilk biscuit

BUTTERMILK BISCUITS

1 = 1 buttermilk roll

CORN TORTILLAS

1 = 1 flour tortilla (burritos)

1 = 1 tostada shell

FLOUR TORTILLAS

1 = 1 pita bread (sandwiches)

PITA BREAD

1 = 1 flour tortilla (sandwiches)

SANDWICH BREAD

1 slice = 1 slice pita bread

WHEAT BREAD

1 slice = 1 slice potato bread

WHITE BREAD

1 slice = 1 slice whole wheat bread

WHITE ROLLS

1 = 1 slice white bread

WHOLE WHEAT BREAD

1 slice = 1 slice rye bread

BREAD CRUMBS

1 cup = 3/4 cup fine cracker crumbs

1 cup = 3/4 cup wheat germ

1 cup = 1 cup whole wheat bread crumbs

1 cup = 1 cup shredded potatoes (meatloaf)

1 cup = 1 cup matza meal (coatings)

1 cup = 1 cup corn flakes (coatings)

1 cup = 1 cup rolled oats (coatings)

1 cup = 1 cup flour (coatings)

1 cup = 1 cup seasoned dried bread sticks

1 cup = 1 cup unseasoned croutons

CROUTONS

1 cup = 1 cup seasoned dried bread sticks

2

BROTHS, SOUPS, & SAUCES

Perhaps you want Chinese food for dinner but have no soy sauce. There are two substitutions for it listed here.

If it's fish you want but have no tartar sauce, you can make your own with a little mayonnaise and pickle relish.

If it's hot sauce you need, you can substitute hot salsa, or you can make your own with some tomato sauce and a few hot red pepper flakes.

BOTTLED BARBECUE SAUCE

1 cup = 1/2 cup barbecue sauce & 1/2 cup catsup (about out)

1 cup = 7/8 cup catsup, 1/8 cup chili powder, 3 tablespoons vinegar, 1 teaspoon garlic powder, & 1 tablespoon paprika

BEEF BOUILLON CUBES

1 cube = 1 teaspoon beef extract

1 cube = 1 teaspoon instant bouillon powder

BEEF BROTH

1 cup = 1 teaspoon beef extract & 1 cup boiling water

1 cup = 1 cup beef stock

1 cup = 1 beef bouillon cube & 1 cup boiling water

1 cup = 1 cup beef soup

1 cup = 1 cup consomme

BEEF SOUP

1 cup = 3/4 cup beef broth, 1 teaspoon beef extract, & 1/4 cup beef stock

BEEF GRAVY

1 cup = 1 cup potato water, 2 beef bouillon cubes, & 2 tablespoons flour

1 cup = 1 cup milk, 2 beef bouillon cubes, & 2 tablespoons flour

BROWN SAUCE

1 cup = 2 beef bouillon cubes, 2 table-spoons flour, 2 tablespoons butter, 1 1/2 cups boiling water, & 1/8 teaspoon salt

CHICKEN BOUILLON CUBES

1 cube = 1/2 cup chicken stock

CHICKEN BROTH

1 cup = 1 cup chicken stock

1 cup = 1 chicken bouillon cube & 1 cup boiling water

1 cup = 1 cup chicken soup

COMMERCIAL CHICKEN SOUP

1 cup = 3/4 cup chicken broth, 1 chicken bouillon cube, & 1/4 cup chicken stock

CHEESE SAUCE

1 cup = 1/2 cup white sauce & 1/2 cup shredded cheese

1 cup = 1 cup cream sauce, 1 1/2 tea-spoon paprika, & 1/4 teaspoon dry mus-tard

CREAM SAUCE

1 cup = 3/4 cup milk, 2 tablespoons flour, 2 tablespoons butter, & 1/4 teaspoon salt

CURRY SAUCE

1 cup = 1 cup white sauce & 1 teaspoon curry

DILL SAUCE

1 cup = 1 cup fennel sauce (for fish)

FISH STOCK

1 cup = 1 cup clam juice

BOTTLED HOLLANDAISE SAUCE

1 cup = 3/4 cup butter, 3 egg yolks, 2 tablespoons lemon juice, & 1/8 teaspoon salt & pepper

HOT PEPPER SAUCE

3/4 cup = 1 small can tomato sauce & a dash red pepper flakes

MILK

1 cup = 1 cup potato water (gravies)

MUSHROOM SAUCE

1 cup = 1 cup cream of mushroom soup

SOY SAUCE

1 tablespoon = 1 tablespoon tamari

1/2 cup = 6 tablespoons Worchester sauce & 2 tablespoons water

MILD TACO SAUCE

1 cup = 1 cup mild salsa

HOT TACO SAUCE

1 cup = 1 cup hot salsa

TOMATO PASTE

1/2 cup = 1 cup tomato sauce (boil down)

TOMATO SAUCE

1 cup = 1/2 cup tomato paste & 1/2 cup water

VEGETABLE BROTH

1 cup = 1 cup milk (gravy)

WHITE SAUCE

1 cup = 3/4 cup milk, 2 tablespoons flour, 2 tablespoons butter, 1/8 teaspoon salt, & a dash pepper

TARTAR SAUCE

1 cup = 2 tablespoons pickle relish & 3/4

mayonnaise

1 cup = 3/4 cup mayonnaise, 2 tablespoons minced pickles, & 1 tablespoon
lemon juice

WORCHESTER SAUCE

1 tablespoon = 1 tablespoon soy sauce,
3-4 drops hot pepper sauce, 1 dash of
sugar, & 3-4 drops lemon juice

MY OWN SUBSTITUTIONS

3

BUTTER & OIL

This chapter has lots of different choices for you, whether your concern is dietary, nutritional, or taste.

If it is just the flavor of butter you desire, there are some amazing products available now that taste like butter. Some are "Butter Buds", "Molly McButter", and "Best of Butter". "Butter Buds", for instance, has only 4 calories per 1/2 teaspoon, no cholesterol, and low sodium content. You can find these at the diet section of your grocery store.

BUTTER

1 cup = 1 cup shortening, 1 teaspoon salt, & 1/2 teaspoon butter flavoring

1 cup = 1 cup vegetable oil & 2 teaspoons salt

1 cup = 1/2 cup butter & 1/2 cup vegetable oil

1 cup = 1 cup corn oil

1 cup = 7/8 cup soy oil

1 cup = 1 cup soy butter

1 cup = 7/8 cup nut oil

1 cup = 7/8 cup cottenseed oil

1 cup = 3/4 cup bacon drippings & 1/4 cup vegetable oil

1 cup = 3/4 cup bacon drippings & 1/4 cup liquid

1 tablespoon = 1/2 teaspoon butter extract

1/2 cup = 1/2 cup olive oil (sauteeing)

1/2 cup = 1/2 cup peanut oil (sauteeing)

1/2 cup = 1/2 cup beef fat (gravy)

1/2 cup = 1/2 cup pork fat (gravy)

1/2 cup = 1/2 cup chicken fat (gravy)

GARLIC BUTTER

1/4 cup = 1 clove garlic & 3 tablespoons butter

PEANUT BUTTER

1 cup = 1 cup tahini

1 cup = 1 cup nut butter

HONEY BUTTER

1/3 cup = 1 tablespoon honey & 4 table-spoons butter

MARGERINE

1 cup = 1 cup shortening, 1 teaspoon salt, & 1/2 teaspoon butter flavoring

1 cup = 1 cup vegetable oil

SOLID SHORTENING

1 cup = 1 cup corn oil

1 cup = 1 cup nut oil

1 cup = 1 cup olive oil (sauteeing)

1 cup = 1 cup peanut oil

1 cup = 1 cup safflower oil

1 cup = 1 cup sesame oil

1 cup = 1 cup soybean oil

1 cup = 1 cup sunflower seed oil

1 cup = 1 cup vegetable oil

1 cup = 1 coating of Pam

VEGETABLE OIL

1 cup = 1 cup soybean oil

1 cup = 1 cup corn oil

1 cup = 1 cup nut oil

1 cup = 1 cup olive oil (sauteeing)

1 cup = 1 cup peanut oil

1 cup = 1 cup rapeseed (canola) oil

1 cup = 1 cup sesame oil

1 cup = 1 cup solid shortening

1 cup = 1 cup safflower oil

1 cup = 1 cup sunflower seed oil

1 cup = 1 cup butter

1 cup = 1 coating of Pam

BACON FAT

1 cup = 1 cup vegetable oil & 1 beef bouillon cube

CORN OIL

1 cup = 1 cup sunflower seed oil

1 cup = 1 cup coconut oil

1 cup = 1 cup safflower oil

PEANUT OIL

1 cup = 1 cup safflower oil

1 cup = 1 cup sunflower seed oil

1 cup = 1 cup sesame seed oil

OLIVE OIL

1 cup = 1/4 cup sliced green olives &
marinated in 3/4 cup corn oil

1 cup = 1 cup soybean oil

1 cup = 1 cup peanut oil

SAFFLOWER OIL

1 cup = 1 cup sunflower seed oil

1 cup = 1 cup peanut oil

SESAME SEED OIL

1 cup = 1 cup peanut oil

1 cup = 1 cup sunflower seed oil

4

CHEESE

Perhaps you want that swiss cheese taste for a sandwich or a casserole, or need mozzarelli cheese to fix pizza. There are several cheeses that closely substitute.

Maybe you picked up mild cheddar cheese at the store rather than sharp. You can make it taste sharp with a little dry mustard and Worchester sauce.

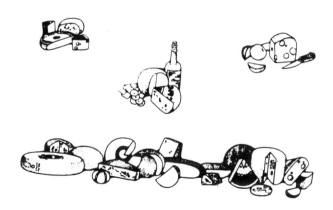

AMERICAN CHEESE

1 cup = 1 cup velveeta cheese

BLUE CHEESE

1 cup = 1 cup gorgonzola cheese

1 cup = 1 cup roquefort cheese

BRIE CHEESE

1 cup = 1 cup camembert cheese

SHARP CHEDDAR CHEESE

1 cup = 1 cup mild cheddar cheese, 1/8 teaspoon dry mustard, & 1/8 teaspoon Worchester sauce

CHEDDAR CHEESE

1 cup = 1 cup cheddar cheese soup

1 cup = 1 cup soy substitute

CHEESE SPREAD

1 cup = 1 cup imitation cheese spread

COTTAGE CHEESE

1 cup = 1 cup feta cheese

1 cup = 1 cup ricotta cheese

1 cup = 1 cup cream cheese

1 cup = 1 cup yogurt (dips)

CREAM CHEESE

1 cup = 1 cup cottage cheese & 4 table-spoons butter (blended)

1 cup = 1 cup neutchatel cheese

1 cup = 1 cup cholesterol free imitation cream cheese

FARMERS CHEESE

1 cup = 1 cup ricotta cheese

1 cup = 1 cup cottage cheese

1 cup = 1 cup cream cheese

FETA CHEESE

1 cup = 1 cup ricotta cheese

1 cup = 1 cup dry curd cottage cheese

1 cup = 1 cup pot cheese

1 cup = 1 cup hoop cheese

1 cup = 1 cup soft Mexican cheese

MILD WHITE CHEESES

1 cup = 1 cup tofu

1 cup = 1 cup soy substitutes

MONTERAY JACK CHEESE

1 cup = 1 cup muenster cheese

1 cup = 1 cup mountain cheese

1 cup = 1 cup mozzarelli cheese

MOZZARELLI CHEESE

1 cup = 1 cup monteray jack cheese

1 cup = 1 cup muenster cheese

1 cup = 1 cup brick cheese

MUENSTER CHEESE

1 cup = 1 cup monteray jack cheese

1 cup = 1 cup mozzarelli cheese

PARMESAN CHEESE

1 cup = 1 cup romano cheese

1 cup = 1 cup Greek kefalotiri cheese

PROVALENE CHEESE

1 cup = 1 cup kasseri cheese

1 cup = 1 cup Turkish kaser cheese

1 cup = 1 cup Bulgarian kashkaval cheese

RICOTTA CHEESE

1 tablespoon = 1 tablespoon cream cheese

1 cup = 1 cup cottage cheese

1 cup = 1 cup farmer cheese

1 cup = 1 cup tofu

ROMANO CHEESE

1 cup = 1 cup parmesan cheese

1 cup = 1 cup Greek kefalotiri cheese

ROQUEFORT CHEESE

1 cup = 1 cup blue cheese

SWISS CHEESE

1 cup = 1 cup jarlsberg cheese

1 cup = 1 cup emmenthalu cheese

1 cup = 1 cup gruyere cheese

TOFU

1 cup = 1 cup lowfat white cheese

VELVEETA CHEESE

1 cup = 1 cup american cheese

5

CHOCOLATE

For those times when you need unsweetened or sweetened chocolate but don't have any, you can make your own with just a few ingredients. If you have either cocoa or carob powder in the cabinet, and sugar, butter, or oil, then you're still in luck.

UNSWEETENED CHOCOLATE

1 square = 3 tablespoons cocoa powder & 2 teaspoons shortening

1 square = 3 tablespoons cocoa powder & 1 tablespoon vegetable oil

1 square = 3 tablespoons cocoa powder & 1 tablespoon butter

1 square = 3 tablespoons carob powder, 1 tablespoon milk, & 1 tablespoon butter

1 square = 3 tablespoons carob powder, 1 tablespoon milk, & 2 teaspoons shortening

1 square = 3 tablespoons carob powder, 1 tablespoon milk, & 1 tablespoon vegetable oil

COCOA POWDER

3 tablespoons = 3 tablespoons carob powder & 1 tablespoon milk

CAROB POWDER

3 tablespoons = 3 tablespoons cocoa powder

CHOCOLATE MILK

1 cup = 1 cup sweetened carob milk

SEMI-SWEET CHOCOLATE

1 square = 3 tablespoons cocoa powder

3 tablespoons sugar, & 1 tablespoon butter

1 square = 3 tablespoons cocoa powder 3 tablespoons sugar, & 2 teaspoons shortening

1 square = 3 tablespoons cocoa powder 3 tablespoons sugar, & 1 tablespoon vegetable oil

1 square = 3 tablespoons carob powder, 3 tablespoons sugar, & 1 tablespoon butter

1 square = 3 tablespoons carob powder, 3 tablespoons sugar, & 2 teaspoons shortening

1 square = 3 tablespoons carob powder, 3 tablespoons sugar, & 1 tablespoon vegetable oil

CHOCOLATE FLAVOR

1 envelope unsweetened baking chocolate flavor

Imitation chocolate flavoring extract

CHOCOLATE FUDGE ICING

3 cups = 1/2 cup fudge topping & 1 canister whipped topping

CHOCOLATE FUDGE

1/3 cup = 2 tablespoons cocoa, 3 tablespoons sugar, & 1/4 cup milk (melt at low)

6

COFFEE, JUICES, & DRINKS

If you are a person who drinks alot of coffee, you may want to keep on hand one of the eight substitutes listed here for when you run out.

Or if you prefer black tea, a close substitution is English tea. There are also alot of herb teas if you prefer a change.

Are you concerned about chemicals in your tap water? Substitute distilled water for an improvement.

You can make your own fruit juice out of fruit puree which is great to drink, or use it in breads and cakes.

Or if your recipe calls for coconut milk, substitute almond milk. Recipes to make your own nut milks are given in Ch. 15.

COFFEE GRAINS

= ground roasted dandelion roots

= ground roasted chicory tap roots

= ground roasted malt grains

= ground roasted barley grains

=ground roasted rye grains

= ground roasted wheat germ

= ground roasted barley, chicory, wild acorns, & rye

= ground roasted azuki beans, black soybeans, brown rice, & dandelion root

EXPRESSO

1 cup = 2 cups coffee

CLUB SODA

1 cup = 1 cup seltzer

1 cup = 1 cup mineral water

CHOCOLATE MILK

1 cup = 1 cup carob milk

COCONUT MILK

1 cup = 1 cup almond milk

COW'S MILK

1 cup = 1 cup goat's milk

TOMATO JUICE

1 cup = 1/2 cup tomato sauce & 1/2 cup water

APPLE JUICE

1 cup = 1/2 cup apple puree, 2 table-spoons sugar, & 1/2 cup water

APRICOT JUICE

1 cup = 1/2 cup apricot puree, 2 table-spoons sugar, & 1/2 cup water

CHERRY PUNCH

1 cup = 1 cup cherry soda

GRAPE JUICE

1 cup = 1/2 cup grape puree, 2 table-spoons sugar, & 1/2 cup water

1 cup = 1 cup grape drink

GRAPEFRUIT JUICE

1 cup = 1/2 cup grapefruit puree, 4 table-spoons sugar, & 1/2 cup water

LIMADE

1 cup = 1 cup gatorade

LIME JUICE

1 cup = 1 cup lemon juice

LEMON JUICE

1 cup = 1 cup artificial lemon drink

1 cup = 1 cup lime juice

MANGO JUICE

1 cup = 1/2 cup mango puree, 2 table-spoons sugar, & 1/2 cup water

CHERRY COOLAID

1 cup = 1 cup cherry punch

ORANGE DRINK

1 cup = 1 cup orange soda

1 cup = 1 cup orange juice

ORANGE JUICE

1 cup = 1 cup orange drink

1 cup = 1/2 cup orange puree, 2 table-spoons sugar, & 1/2 cup water

PAPAYA JUICE

1 cup = 1/2 cup papaya puree, 3 table-spoons sugar, & 1/2 cup water

PEACH JUICE

1 cup = 1/2 cup peach puree, 2 table-spoons sugar, & 1/2 cup water

PEAR JUICE

1 cup = 1 cup apple juice (cooking)

1 cup = 1/2 cup pear puree, 2 table-spoons sugar, & 1/2 cup water

PINNEAPPLE JUICE

1 cup = 1/2 cup pinneapple puree, 3 tablespoons sugar, & 1/2 cup water

FRUIT PUNCH

1 cup = 1 cup cherry coolaid

1 cup = 1 cup artificial fruit drink

6 cups = 1/2 cup apple puree, 1/2 cup coconut puree, 1/2 cup pinneapple puree, 1/2 cup pear puree, 1/2 cup peach puree, 1/2 cup cherry puree, 1 cup sugar, & 2 cups water (strained & modified if necessary)

SELTZER

1 cup = 1 cup mineral water

1 cup = 1 cup club soda

BLACK TEA

1 cup = 1 cup english tea

1 cup = 1 cup sassafras tea

1 cup = 1 cup herb teas

1 cup = 1 cup black walnut tea

1 cup = 1 cup ginseng tea

1 cup = 1 cup gotu kola tea

1 cup = 1 cup cammomile tea

1 cup = 1 cup licorice root tea

1 cup = 1 cup fruit & almond tea

1 cup = 1 cup lady slipper tea

1 cup = 1 cup chickweed tea

1 cup = 1 cup fennel tea

1 cup = 1 cup valerian root tea

TAP WATER

1 cup = 1 cup distilled water

1 cup = 1 cup mineral water

MY OWN SUBSTITUTIONS

7

DAIRY

Heavy cream can be made light, and light cream can be made heavy. There are many substitutions given for sour cream, buttermilk, and sour milk. If you need sour milk in a recipe, it can be made sour.

Yogurt when used as a substitute should not be boiled as it may separate, as will sour cream, therefore a different substitution would be recommended in this situation.

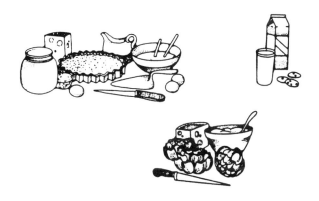

SOUR CREAM

1 cup = 3/4 cup milk & 3 tablespoons mayonnaise

1 cup = 1 cup plain yogurt

1 cup = 1 cup buttermilk

1 cup = 3/4 cup sour milk & 1/4 cup melted butter

1 cup = 1 cup fresh cream & 1 table-spoon lemon juice

1 cup = 1 cup cottage cheese pureed & 1 teaspoon lemon juice

1 cup = 1/3 cup cottage cheese pureed, 1/3 cup yogurt, 2 tablespoons milk, & 1 tablespoon lemon juice

1 cup = 3/4 cup cream cheese & 1/4 cup water

1 cup = 3/4 cup cream cheese & 1/4 cup milk

1 cup = 1/2 cup soya milk, 1/4 cup vine-gar, & 1/3 cup cornstarch

1 cup = 7/8 cup evaporated milk & 1 ta-blespoon vinegar (let stand 5 min)

1 cup = 7/8 cup evaporated milk & 1 ta-blespoon lemon juice

1 cup = 1 cup low calorie imitation sour cream

BUTTERMILK

1 cup = 1 cup plain yogurt

1 cup = 1 cup sour milk

1 cup = 1 cup milk & 1 3/4 teaspoon cream of tartar

1 cup = 1/2 cup evaporated milk, 1/2 cup water, & 1 tablespoon vinegar (let stand 10 min)

1 cup = 1/2 cup evaporated milk, 1/2 cup water, & 1 tablespoon lemon juice (let stand 10 min)

1 cup = 1 cup warm milk & 1 tablespoon vinegar (let stand 10 min)

1 cup = 1 cup warm milk & 1 tablespoon lemon juice (let stand 10 min)

1 cup = 1 cup sour cream

COCONUT CREAM

1 cup = 1 cup light cream & 1 teaspoon coconut extract

YOGURT

1 cup = 1 cup sour milk

1 cup = 1 cup buttermilk

1 cup = 1 cup sour cream

1 cup = 1 cup creme fraiche

1 cup = 1 cup heavy cream

1/2 cup = 1/2 cup mayonnaise (dips)

1 cup = 1/3 cup soya milk powder, 1 cup heated water & 1 teaspoon yogurt (keep same heat 3 hours) (about out)

FLAVORED YOGURT

1 cup = 1/2 cup plain yogurt & 1/2 cup pureed fruit

SOUR MILK

1 cup = 1 cup plain yogurt

1 cup = 1 cup buttermilk

1 cup = 1/2 cup evaporated milk, 1/2 cup water, & 1 tablespoon vinegar (let stand 10 min)

1 cup = 1/2 cup evaporated milk, 1/2 cup water, & 1tablespoon lemon juice (let stand 10 min)

1 cup = 1 cup warm milk & 1 tablespoon vinegar (let stand 10 min)

1 cup = 1 cup warm milk & 1 tablespoon lemon juice (let stand 10 min)

HEAVY CREAM

1 cup = 2/3 cup milk & 1/3 cup melted butter

1 cup = 2 cups whipping cream

1 cup = 3/4 cup milk & 1/4 cup vegetable oil

HEAVY WHIPPED CREAM

1 cup = 2/3 cup chilled evaporated milk whipped

LIGHT CREAM

1 cup = 3/4 cup milk & 1/4 cup melted butter

1 cup = 1/2 cup milk & 1/2 cup whipping cream

1 cup = 1/2 cup milk & 1/2 cup heavy cream

1 cup = 1/2 cup evaporated milk, 1/3 cup whole milk, & 2 tablespoons butter

1 cup = 1 cup coconut cream

1 cup = 1 cup low fat imitation cream

WHIPPING CREAM

1 cup = 2 cups desert topping

1 cup = 1 cup half & half

1 cup = 2/3 cup chilled evaporated milk whipped

CREAM FRAICHE

1 cup = 1 cup sour cream & dash baking soda

DESSERT TOPPING

   1 cup = 1 cup flavored yogurt

FLAVORED JELLO

   1 3 oz package = 1 envelope plain gelatin & 2 cups fruit juice

   MY OWN SUBSTITUTIONS

8

DESSERTS

If it's a craving for a candy bar that comes over you, then you know there is nothing worse. But you can simulate your favorite tastes if you have peanuts, peanut butter, chocolate chips, caramelle squares, or coconut in your baking cabinet.

If it's chocolate ice cream you want as a topping for that chocolate cake you just baked, you'll be surprised what a nice substitute chilled whipped topping mixed with fudge topping makes.

CHERRY PUDDING

1 cup = 1 cup vanilla pudding & 1 table-spoon grenadine syrup

CINNAMON ROLLS

1 roll = 2 slices cinnamon toast & 2 table-spoons white icing

CHOCOLATE ICE CREAM

1 cup = 1 cup chocolate This Can't Be Yogurt

1 cup = 3/4 cup whipped topping & 1/4 cup chocolate fudge topping (cake toppings)

VANILLA ICE CREAM

1 cup = 1 cup vanilla Braums frozen yogurt

MOST FLAVORS ICE CREAM

1 cup = 1 cup same flavor This Can't Be Yogurt

FROZEN FRUIT STICKS

1 stick = 1/2 cup fruit in 1/2 cup vanilla ice cream

CHERRY POPSICLES

1 popsicle = 3 fruit punch ice cubes

POPSICLES

1 popsicle = 3 coolaid ice cubes

1 popsicle = 3 fruit juice ice cubes

ORANGE POPSICLES

1 orange popsicle = 3 orange juice cubes

HERSHEYS CHOCOLATE CANDY BARS

1 bar = 1/2 cup Hersheys Kisses

REESES PEANUT BUTTER CUPS

1 cup = 1 tablespoon peanut butter & 2 tablespoons chocolate chips

1 cup = 1 tablespoon peanut butter & 1 tablespoon homemade chocolate

HERSHEYS GOODBAR

1 bar = 1/3 cup Hersheys Kisses & 1/4 cup peanuts

1 bar = 1/3 cup chocolate chips & 1/4 cup peanuts

CARAMELLE BARS

1 bar = 1/4 cup chocolate chips & 1/4 cup Kraft caramel squares

1 bar = 1/4 cup Hersheys Kisses & 1/4 cup Kraft caramel squares

9

DIPS, DRESSINGS, & SPREADS

What can you do when dinner is served and you reach for the salad dressing only to find it's not there!   If you can wait five more minutes, you will be able to throw together one of the salad dressing recipes in this chapter and make your own.

If it's mustard, catsup, or mayonnaise you need, there's something you can do. There are 4 substitutions for mayonnaise, 3 for catsup, and 2 for mustard.

COMMERCIAL BEAN DIP

1 cup = 1 cup crushed pinto beans, 1 teaspoon paprika, 1 teaspoon salt, 1 teaspoon coriander, & a dash of hot sauce

BOTTLED BLUE CHEESE DRESSING

1 cup = 2/3 cup plain yogurt, 1/3 cup mayonnaise, 1/3 cup blue cheese, 1/4 cup milk, & 1/3 cup cottage cheese

CATSUP

1 tablespoon = 1 tablespoon steak sauce (hamburgers)

1 cup = 3/4 cup tomato sauce, 1 1/2 tablespoons vinegar, 1/4 cup sugar, & 1/4 teaspoon ground cloves

1 cup = 3/4 cup tomato sauce, 1 1/2 tablespoons vinegar, & 1/4 cup sugar

BOTTLED CREAM SALAD DRESSING

1 cup = 1 cup mayonnaise & choice of 1/2 teaspoon pepper, 1/2 teaspoon salt, 1/2 teaspoon green pepper flakes, 1/2 teaspoon paprika, 1/2 teaspoon onion powder, 1/2 teaspoon garlic powder, 1/2 teaspoon curry, 1/2 teaspoon cinnamon, 1/2 teaspoon mace, and 1/2 teaspoon ginger

BOTTLED FRENCH DRESSING

1 cup = 7/8 cup salad oil, 2 teaspoons sugar, 4 tablespoons vinegar, 1 teaspoon salt, 2 teaspoons dry mustard, 1/4 teaspoon paprika, & 2 drops hot sauce

COMMERCIAL FRENCH ONION DIP

1 cup = 1 cup sour cream, 1 tablespoon finely chopped onions, 1 tablespoon parsley, 1/2 teaspoon salt, & 1/2 teaspoon garlic

BOTTLED GREEN GODDESS DRESSING

1 cup = 1/3 cup mayonnaise, 1/3 cup sour cream, 1/8 cup milk, 1/2 cup parsley, 1/3 cup chopped green onion, 1 1/2 tablespoons tarragon wine vinegar, 1/4 teaspoon basil, 1/8 teaspoon sugar, & 1/2 teaspoon anchovy paste

BOTTLED HORSERADISH

2 tablespoons = 1 tablespoon fresh horseradish

2 tablespoons = 1 teaspoon dry horseradish & 1 tablespoon water

BOTTLED ITALIAN DRESSING

1 cup = 2/3 cup salad oil, 1/4 cup white

vinegar, 1 teaspoon minced garlic, 1/8 cup parmesan cheese, 1/8 teaspoon paprika, 1/2 teaspoon sugar, 1 teaspoon salt, 1/4 teaspoon pepper, 1/2 teaspoon celery leaves, 1 teaspoon parsley, & 1/4 teaspoon dry mustard

MAYONNAISE

2 cups = 3 tablespoons powdered milk, 1/2 cup vegetable oil, 1/2 cup water, 1 teaspoon sugar, 1/2 teaspoon garlic salt, 1/2 teaspoon onion salt, & 1/2 teaspoon paprika. Blend. Add 1/2 cup vegetable oil & 1/4 cup lemon juice until thick.

2 cups = 3 tablespoons soya milk powder, 1/2 cup vegetable oil, 1/2 cup water, 1 teaspoon sugar, 1/2 teaspoon garlic salt, 1/2 teaspoon onion salt, & 1/2 teaspoon paprika. Blend. Add 1/2 cup vegetable oil & 1/4 cup lemon juice until thick.

1 cup = 1 cup yogurt

1 cup = 1 cup sour cream (dips)

BOTTLED MUSTARD

1 tablespoon = 1 tablespoon dry mustard, 1 teaspoon vinegar, & 2 teaspoons water

1 tablespoon = 1 teaspoon dry mustard, 1 teaspoon wine, & 2 teaspoons water

BOTTLED POPPY SEED DRESSING

1 cup = 2/3 cup salad oil, 1/4 cup chopped onion, 1/4 cup white vinegar, 1 1 tablespoon poppy seed, 1/2 cup sugar, 1 teaspoon dry mustard, 1/2 teaspoon salt, & 1/8 teaspoon pepper

BOTTLED THOUSAND ISLAND DRESSING

1 cup = 1/2 cup mayonnaise, 1/8 cup milk 1/2 cup chopped hard boiled eggs, 1 tablespoon chopped onions, 1 tablespoon chopped green pepper, 1 tablespoon celery leaves, 1/8 cup chili powder, & 1/4 teaspoon salt

BOTTLED VINEGAR & OIL DRESSING

1 cup = 3/4 cup olive oil, 2 tablespoons lemon juice, & 1/4 cup parsley

MY OWN SUBSTITUTIONS

10

EGGS

Eggs are used to make food stick together in cooking as well as for flavor.

If it's flavor you want, perhaps you may want to choose mayonnaise as a substitute. If it is thickness in a sauce or soup, you may choose plain gelatin or blended apricots.

Flaxseed or xanthan gum can be purchased from a health food store and kept in your cabinet as excellent substitutes to be used in a bind.

EGGS

1 egg = 2 tablespoons mayonnaise

1 egg = 1 teaspoon cornstarch & 3 tablespoons water

1 egg = 1 teaspoon baking soda, 2 tablespoons water, & 1 teaspoon cornstarch

1 egg= 1 tablespoon flour, 1 tablespoon water, 1 tablespoon oil, & 1 teaspoon baking powder

1 egg= 2 tablespoons dried egg, & 2 tablespoons water

1 egg= 2 tablespoons vegetable oil & 1 tablespoon water

1 egg = 2 tablespoons blended apricots (soups, sauces)

1 egg = 1 tablespoon apricot puree & 1 tablespoon banana puree (soups, sauces)

1 egg = 1 teaspoon plain gelatin & 2 tablespoons water (soups, sauces)

1 egg = 1 tablespoon commercial egg substitute

1 egg = 3 egg whites, 1 tablespoon powdered milk, 1 tablespoon vegetable oil, & 3 drops yellow food coloring

1 egg = 1 tablespoon flaxseed

1 egg = 2 egg yolks & 1 tablespoon water

1 egg = 2 egg whites

1 egg = 2 egg yolks

1 egg = 1 serving Fleishmans Eggbeaters

1 egg = 1 teaspoon xanthan gum

MY OWN SUBSTITUTIONS

11

FRUITS

No one fruit tastes exactly like another, and some substitutes will come closer than others. It really depends on what you are cooking as to whether a fruit substitute will do.

If it's blueberry pie that you must have, then that is what it has to be. But you may find blackberry or huckleberry pie just as tasty.

If your cookies call for dates, you can use dried currants, figs, or raisens with no difficulty.

Pomegranetes taste similar to cherries, and kiwi fruit taste similar to pears. Limes do well in place of lemons. Nectarines substitute for peaches.

APPLES

1 cup fresh = 1 cup dried

1 cup diced = 1 cup diced pears & 1 tablespoon lemon juice

1 apple = 1 tomatillo

APRICOTS

1 apricot = 1 mango

1 cup fresh = 1 cup dried

1 apricot = 1 kiwi fruit

BANANAS

1 fresh = 1 dried

1 banana = 1 plantain

BLACKBERRIES

1 cup = 1 cup raspberries

1 cup = 1 cup blueberries

1 cup = 1 cup boysenberries

BLUEBERRIES

1 cup = 1 cup blackberries

1 cup = 1 cup boysenberries

BOYSENBERRIES

1 cup = 1 cup blackberries

1 cup = 1 cup raspberries

CANTALOPE

1 cantalope = 4 mangoes

1 cantalope = 1 honeydew melon

CURRANTS

1 cup = 1 cup dates

1 cup = 1 cup prunes

1 cup = 1 cup raisens

DATES

1 cup = 1 cup raisens

1 cup = 1 cup dried currants

1 cup = 1 cup pitted prunes

1 cup = 1 cup figs

PURPLE GRAPES

1 cup = 1 cup red

RED GRAPES

1 cup = 1 cup purple

1 cup = 1 cup white

WHITE GRAPES

1 cup = 1 cup red

HONEYDEW MELON

1 melon = 1 casaba melon

1 melon = 1 cantalope

1 melon = 8 mangoes

1 melon = 3-4 papayas

HUCKLEBERRIES

1 cup = 1 cup blueberries

KIWI FRUIT

1 fruit = 1 apricot

LEMON

1 whole = 3 tablespoons lemon juice & 2 tablespoons dried lemon peel

1 lemon = 1 lime

LIME

1 whole = 2 tablespoons lime juice & 2 tablespoons dried lime peel

1 whole = 2 tablespoons lime juice & 2 tablespoons dried lemon peel

1 whole = 2 tablespoons lemon juice & 2 tablespoons dried lemon peel

1 lime = 1 lemon

MANGO

1 mango = 1 peach

1 mango = 1 apricot

1 mango = 1 papaya

1 cup = 1 cup cantalope

NECTARINES

1 nectarine = 1 peach

ORANGES

1 cup = 1 cup mandarin oranges

1 orange = 1 tangerine

MANDARIN ORANGES

1 orange = 6-7 tablespoons orange juice & 2-3 tablespoons orange peel

1 orange = 6-7 tablespoons tangerine juice & 2-3 tablespoons dried orange peel

MANDARIN ORANGES

2 mandarin oranges = 1 tangerine

2 mandarin oranges = 1 orange

PAPAYA

1 papaya = 1 mango

PEACHES

1 peach = 1 mango

1 peach = 1 sapodilla

1 peach = 1 nectarine

PEARS

1 pear = 1 kiwi fruit

1 pear = 1 apple (pies)

PINNEAPPLE

1 cup = 1 cup mangoes

POMEGRANETES

1 pomegranete = 1 cup cherries

PRUNES

1 cup = 1 cup raisens

1 cup = 1 cup dried currants

1 cup = 1 cup black figs

1 cup = 1 cup dates

RAISENS

1 cup = 1 cup black figs

1 cup = 1 cup dried currants

1 cup = 1 cup dates

1 cup = 1 cup prunes

RASPBERRIES

1 cup = 1 cup boysenberries

1 cup = 1 cup blackberries

1 cup = 1 cup strawberries

TANGERINES

1 tangerine = 2 mandarin oranges

12

LEAVENING AGENTS

The two most common missing ingredients in the kitchen when it comes to leavening agents are yeast and baking powder.

If you have some cream of tartar, cornstarch, and baking soda in your cabinet, you've got a substitute for baking powder. If you have no cream of tartar, there is a substitution that calls for sour milk or buttermilk, baking soda, and cornstarch. If you have no sour milk, there is a way to make it sour. (See Ch. 7)

ACTIVE DRY YEAST

1 package = 1 teaspoon baking powder

1 package = 1/2 cup sour dough starter

1 package = 1 6 oz cake compressed yeast

BAKING POWDER

1 teaspoon = 2 teaspoons tartrate baking powder

1 teaspoon = 1/2 teaspoon phosphate baking powder

1 teaspoon = 1/4 teaspoon baking soda & 1/2 teaspoon cream of tartar

1 teaspoon = 1/4 teaspoon baking soda, 1/2 teaspoon cream of tartar, & 1/4 teaspoon cornstarch

1 teaspoon = 1/4 teaspoon baking soda, 1/4 teaspoon cornstarch, & 1/2 cup buttermilk (reduce recipe liquid by 1/2 cup)

1 teaspoon = 1/4 teaspoon baking soda, 1/2 cup sour milk, & 1/4 teaspoon cornstarch (reduce recipe liquid by 1/2 cup)

13

MEAT

There are many types of meats, fish, and poultry that substitute for others.

Crayfish substitutes for lobster.

Cod substitutes for ocean perch.

Ham substitutes for Canadian Bacon.

Cornish Game hen salad substitutes for chicken salad.

Tuna substitutes for sardines.

Many people use eggplant instead of beef.

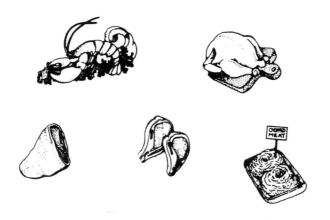

BACON

= pepperoni (sandwiches)

= dried bacon bits

= packaged real bacon bits

BASS

= swordfish

= bluefish

FRIED BASS

= fried chicken

BEEF

= eggplant

BOLOGNA

= salami

= spam

BOTTOM ROUND STEAK

= round tip roast

CANADIAN BACON

= ham

CATFISH

= bass

FRIED CATFISH

= fried chicken

CAVIAR

= salmon roe

= lumpfish roe

CHICKEN

= cornish game hen

= canned turkey

= rabbit

CHICKEN SALAD

= cornish game hen salad

= turkey salad

CHUCK ROAST

= rump roast

CHUCK ARM POT ROAST

= chuck blade roast

= chuck eye roast

CHUCK BLADE ROAST

= chuck eye roast

CHUCK EYE ROAST

= chuck blade roast

= chuck arm pot roast

CHUCK SHORT RIBS

= plate ribs

CLAMS

= couch

= cockles

COD

= halibut

= ocean perch

CORN BEEF

= canned corn beef hash

CORNISH GAME HEN

= quail

= chicken

CRAB

= canned turkey (casseroles)

= canned tuna (casseroles)

= canned chicken (casseroles)

CRAYFISH

= lobster

DUCK

= roasting hen

COMMERCIAL EGGROLLS

= 1 can crab meat, 1 cup shredded cabbage, 1/2 tablespoon soy sauce, 1/2 teaspoon salt, 1/2 teaspoon pepper, & 1 teaspoon garlic powder. Fry in thin dough.

FLANK STEAK ROLLS

= rolled flank steak

GOAT

=mutton

GOOSE LIVERS

= chicken livers

GROUND BEEF

= ground turkey

= soy-meat blend

= ground veal

GROUND PORK

= sausage

= ground turkey

GROUND LAMB

= ground veal

GROUND CHUCK

= ground round

GROUND ROUND

= ground chuck

GROUND VEAL

= ground lamb

HALIBUT

= trout

= cod

HAM

= turkey ham

= canadian bacon (sandwiches)

HOT DOGS

= Italian sausage

= Polish sausage

= German sausage

= vienna sausage

= turkey dogs

ITALIAN SAUSAGE

= 1 hot dog, 1/8 teaspoon cumin, & 1/8 teaspoon garlic powder stuffed down center

LOBSTER

= crayfish

MACKERAL

   = salmon

   = tuna

MEAT SUBSTITUTE

   = soybeans

NEW YORK STRIP STEAK

   = rib eye steak

OCEAN PERCH

   = cod

   = hake

PEPPERONI

   = bacon

PLATE RIBS

   = chuck short ribs

POLISH SAUSAGE

   = hot dogs

   = German sausage

PORK CHOPS

= lamb chops

PORTERHOUSE STEAK

= top loin steak

RABBIT

= chicken

RIB EYE STEAK

= KC steak

= round steak

RIB ROAST

= Rib eye roast (Delmonico)

ROLLED FLANK STEAK

= scored flank steak

ROUND TIP ROAST

= bottom round steak

SALAMI

= Bologna sprinkled with garlic & black peppercorns

SALT PORK

= pig's tails

SARDINES

= mackeral

= tuna

SCORED FLANK STEAK

= flank steak rolls

SHANK CROSSCUTS

= chuck short ribs

= plate ribs

SAUSAGE

= ground pork

SHELLFISH

= pacific whitefish

SHRIMP

= catfish (casseroles)

= tuna (casseroles)

= chicken (casseroles)

SPAM

= bologna

SQUAB

= cornish game hen

SQUID

= couch

STUFFED GREEN PEPPERS

= stuffed eggplant

TOP LOIN STEAK

= porterhouse steak

TOP ROUND STEAK

= bottom rip roast

= round rib roast

TROUT

= pompano

= halibut

TUNA

= mackeral

= sardines

= chicken (casseroles)

= canned turkey (casseroles)

= crab

TURKEY

= turkey legs (casseroles)

= canned chicken (casseroles)

VEAL BONELESS SHOULDER ROAST

= veal arm roast

VEAL LEG ROUND ROAST

= veal leg round steak

VEAL LOIN CHOP

= veal loin roast

VEAL LOIN ROAST

= veal loin kidney chop

VEAL ARM STEAK

= veal boneless shoulder roast

VEAL SCALOPPINI

= turkey breasts

= chicken breasts

= eggplant

VENISON CHOPS

= rump roast

VENISON SHOULDER

= venison steak

VIENNA SAUSAGE

= polish sausage

= hot dogs

= bologna

= German sausage

MY OWN SUBSTITUTIONS

14

MILK

Milk is a common ingredient that comes up missing from your refrigerator. There are many substitutions for whole milk, and also substitutions for skim milk and chocolate milk, etc., in this chapter.

If you need coconut milk, you can make your own with light cream and coconut extract, or you can substitute almond milk, which you can make yourself. (See Ch. 15)

Fruit or vegetable juice can be substituted for milk in breads and cakes with good results.

WHOLE MILK

1 cup = 1/2 cup evaporated milk & 1/2 cup water

1 cup = 1/4 cup powdered milk & 1 cup water

1 cup = 1/4 cup powdered milk, 1 cup water, & 2 teaspoons butter

1 cup = 1 cup buttermilk & 1/2 teaspoon baking soda

1 cup = 1/2 cup coffee creamer & 3/4 cup water

1 cup = 1 cup skim milk & 2 tablespoons butter

1 cup = 1 cup light cream

1 cup = 1/4 cup soya milk powder & 1 cup water

1 cup = 1/4 cup soya milk powder, 1/2 teaspoon vanilla, & 1 cup water

1 cup = 1 cup soya milk (mix 1 cup seived soybeans, 1 tablespoon sugar, 1/8 teaspoon salt, 1/2 cup water, & 1/2 teaspoon vanilla)

1 cup = 1 cup oat milk (puree 1/3 cup rolled oats, 1 teaspoon honey, & 1 cup water

1 cup = 1 cup fruit juice (breads, cakes)

1 cup = 1 cup fruit puree (breads, cakes)

1 cup = 1 cup vegetable juice (breads, cakes)

1 cup = 1 cup vegetable puree (breads, cakes)

SKIM MILK

1 cup = 1/2 cup whole milk & 1/2 cup water

1 cup = 1/2 cup evaporated milk & 1/2 cup water

COCONUT MILK

1 cup = 1 cup almond milk

1 cup = 1 cup whole milk & 1 teaspoon coconut extract

1 cup = 1 cup light cream & 1 teaspoon coconut extract

CHOCOLATE MILK

1 cup = 1 cup sweetened carob milk

MY OWN SUBSTITUTIONS

15

NUT MILKS

If you are out of milk, and are preparing cakes, breads, or cookies that also call for nuts, you can make a number of nut milks with a blender that will work quite well.

Nut milks are good sources of protein from a nutritional viewpoint, and can be used in place of other sources of equivalent protein.

WHOLE MILK

1 cup = 1 cup nut milk

1 cup = 1 cup sesame milk (puree 1 tablespoon sesame seeds, 1 teaspoon honey, 1 teaspoon lemon juice, & 1 cup water

1 cup = 1 cup almond milk (puree 1 tablespoon sweet almonds, 1 teaspoon honey, & 1 cup water)

1 cup = 1 cup almond milk (stir 1 teaspoon melted sweet almond butter, 1 teaspoon honey, & 1 cup water)

1 cup = 1 cup pine milk (puree 1 tablespoon pine nuts, 1 teaspoon honey, & 1 cup water)

1 cup = 1 cup walnut milk (puree 1 tablespoon walnuts, 1 teaspoon honey, & 1 cup water)

1 cup = 1 cup cashew milk (puree 1 tablespoon cashews, 1 teaspoon honey, & 1 cup water)

16

NUTS

Many nuts can be substituted for each other.

Sunflower seeds have that peanutty taste, and almonds can substitute for cashews in such dishes as "Cashew Chicken".

Nut extracts are good substitutes such as sweet almond or walnut extract when flavor is desired.

Bran can be substituted for nuts in cakes.

SWEET ALMONDS

1 cup = 1 cup hazelnuts

1 cup = 1 cup chironji nuts

1 tablespoon ground = 1 tablespoon sweet almond extract

CASHEWS

1 cup = 1 cup almonds

PEANUTS

1 cup = 1 cup sunflower seeds

1 cup = 1 cup soy nuts

PECANS

1 cup = 1 cup almonds

1 cup = 1 cup walnuts

PINE NUTS

1 cup = 1 cup sunflower seeds

1 cup = 1 cup sweet almonds

1 cup = 1 cup walnuts

WALNUTS

1 tablespoon ground = 1 tablespoon walnut extract

NUTS

1 cup = 1 cup bran (cakes)

17

PASTA, NOODLES, & SPAGHETTI

The making of pasta is a mystery to most of us, but believe it or not you can make your own noodles or spaghetti if you run out. It's easy with a little flour of your choice, an egg, some salt and water.

If you prefer to use ready made noodles as substitutions for other noodles, the substitution will be close. Many noodles differ only in their shape or size, but are made from the same thing.

ANGEL HAIR PASTA

1 cup = 1 cup vermicelli

PASTA

1 cup = 1 cup oriental ramen noodles

1 cup = 1 eggplant

RICE VERMICELLI

1 cup = 1 cup angel hair pasta

1 cup = 1 cup rice flour noodles

1 cup = 1 cup spaghettini

1 cup = 1 cup mung bean flour noodles

1 cup = 1 cup Japanese ramen noodles

NOODLES

1 cup = 1 cup rice flour, 1 egg, 1/4 cup water, & 1/2 teaspoon salt (sliced, dried, & boiled)

1 cup = 1 cup oat flour, 1 egg, 1/4 cup water, & 1/2 teaspoon salt (sliced, dried, & boiled)

1 cup = 1 cup buckwheat flour, 1 egg, 1/4 cup water, & 1/2 teaspoon salt (sliced, dried, & boiled)

1 cup = 1 cup Chinese bean threads

1 cup = 1 cup corn flour, 1 egg, 1/4 cup water, & 1/2 teaspoon salt (sliced, dried, & boiled)

1 cup = 1 cup amaranth flour, 1 egg, 1/4 cup water, & 1/2 teaspoon salt (sliced, dried, & boiled)

LASAGNA NOODLES

1 cup = 1 cup small noodles

COOKED SPAGHETTI

1 cup = 1 cup rice flour, 1 egg, 1/4 cup water, & 1/2 teaspoon salt (sliced, dried, & boiled)

1 cup = 1 cup corn flour, 1 egg, 1/4 cup water, & 1/2 teaspoon salt (sliced, dried, & boiled)

1 cup = 1 cup oat flour, 1 egg, 1/4 cup water, & 1/2 teaspoon salt (sliced, dried, & boiled)

1 cup = 1 cup amaranth flour, 1 egg, 1/4 cup water, & 1/2 teaspoon salt (sliced, dried, & boiled)

1 cup = 1 cup buckwheat flour, 1 egg, 1/4 cup water, & 1/2 teaspoon salt (sliced, dried, & boiled)

1 cup = 1 cup Chinese bean threads

1 cup = 1 cup vermicelli

18

PET FOODS

Birds love seeds, rice, and bread. Hamsters and mice love seeds and lettuce. Rabbits and guinea pigs love vegetables. Dogs, of course, will eat almost anything. Cats, on the other hand, are notoriously finicky.

One way to trick a cat into eating something besides his/her favorite dish, is to stir the food to release it's smell so that it smells fresh to him. (This also works on food that has been sitting for awhile)

It should be noted that any substitution for your pet should be used as a temporary food only, as it may not contain the nutritional requirements your pet needs on a daily basis.

BIRD SEED

1 cup = 1 cup sunflower seeds

1 cup = 1 cup cooked rice

1 cup = 1 cup bread crumbs

CAT FOOD

1 can = 1/2 can cat food & 1/2 cup rice (about out)

1 can = 1/8 cup diced carrots, 1/8 cup diced potatoes, 1/8 cup diced peas, & 1/2 cup leftover beef (use drippings to mix)

1 can = 1/3 cup cooked rice, 1/3 cup diced potatoes, & 1/3 cup leftover chicken skin (do not boil away grease as the pet will not eat what he/she can not smell)

1 can = 1/3 cup diced potatoes, 1/3 cup peas, & 1/3 cup chopped beef fat (use drippings to mix)

1 can = 1/2 cup chopped boiled eggs, 1/4 slice of velveeta cheese, & 1/16 cup bacon drippings (mix well)

RABBIT PELLETS

1 cup = 1 cup guinea pig pellets

GUINEA PIG PELLETS

1 cup = 1 cup rabbit pellets (add Vit. C)

19

PIE CRUSTS

Some people like to buy their pie crusts ready made, or pick up a Jiffy pie mix and just add water.

For those who prefer to make their own, but have run out of flour or shortening, you can crush cereal flakes, nuts, or even seeds, use a little sugar, water, butter or oil, and you will get a delicious crust.

PIE CRUSTS

1 crust = 1 graham cracker pie crust

1 crust = 1 1/2 cup crushed cornflakes, 2 tablespoons sugar, & 1/3 cup butter

1 crust = 1 1/2 cup crushed rice flakes, 2 tablespoons sugar, & 1/3 cup butter

1 crust = 1 1/2 cup ground nuts, 2 tablespoons sugar, 1/4 cup water, & 1/4 cup butter

1 crust = 1 1/2 cup ground sunflower seeds, 2 tablespoons sugar, 1/4 cup water, & 8 tablespoons oil

1 crust = 1 1/2 cup crushed rye crisp, 2 tablespoons sugar, 1/4 cup water, & 1/3 cup oil

1 crust = 1 1/2 cup crushed matzo, 3 tablespoons sugar, 1/4 cup water, & 1/3 cup oil

20

RICE, CEREAL, & SNACKS

Many people don't know you can substitute popped rice for popcorn or puffed millet for puffed rice as a cereal.

If you run out of white rice, you can use brown rice, kasha, or bulgar. (Cooking times may vary. See the specific substitution.)

If you like to munch on sunflower seeds, you may find pumpkin or squash seeds a delightful substitute.

WHITE RICE

1 cup = 1 cup brown rice (increase cooking time 20-30 min)

1 cup = 1 cup bulgar (increase cooking time 20-30 min)

BROWN RICE

1 cup = 1 cup white rice (decrease cooking time 20-30 min)

1 cup = 1 cup kasha

BULGAR

1 cup = 1 cup cracked wheat

WILD RICE

1 cup = 1/2 cup brown rice & 1/2 cup kasha

TAPIOCA

1 cup = 2 tablespoons rice flour , 1 teaspoon vanilla, & 3 cups milk (boil until thick, then chill)

PUFFED RICE

1 cup = 1 cup puffed millet

OATMEAL

1 cup = 1 cup millet

CREAM OF WHEAT

   1 cup = 1 cup farina

POPPED RICE

   1 cup = 1 cup popcorn

POPCORN

   1 cup = 1 cup popped rice

   1 cup yellow = 1 cup colored popcorn

   1 cup white = 1 cup yellow popcorn

PUMPKIN SEEDS

   1 cup = 1 cup sunflower seeds

SUNFLOWER SEEDS

   1 cup = 1 cup pumpkin seeds

POTATO CHIPS

   1 cup = 1 cup potato sticks

   1 cup = 1 cup fried pork rinds

POTATO STICKS

   1 cup = 1 cup potato chips

TORTILLA CHIPS

   1 cup = 2 crumbled taco shells

   1 cup = 2 crumbled tostada shells

21

SALT

Whether you need to reduce your salt intake, or whether you just ran out, there are many substitutes for you that you may even like better than the original.

Savory, for instance, can be substituted for salt or pepper, and gives a mildly hot taste like pepper does.

Many herb combinations are presented for different foods such as poultry, meat, vegetables, fish, etc. which are also used to spice up your food.

SALT

1 teaspoon = 1 teaspoon powdered kelp

1 teaspoon = 1 teaspoon Kosher salt

1 teaspoon = 1 teaspoon sea salt

1 teaspoon = 1 teaspoon spicy lemon juice

1 teaspoon = 1 teaspoon smoke flavored salt

1 teaspoon = 1 teaspoon pure pickling salt

1 teaspoon = 1 teaspoon Herbs seasoning salt

1 teaspoon = 1 teaspoon herbs

1 teaspoon = 1 teaspoon savory

1 teaspoon = 1 teaspoon mustard powder

1 teaspoon = 1 teaspoon garlic powder

1 teaspoon = 1 teaspoon onion powder

1 teaspoon = 1 teaspoon paprika

1 teaspoon = 1 teaspoon red pepper

1 teaspoon = 1 teaspoon commercial salt substitute

SEASONED SALT SUBSTITUTES

1 teaspoon = 1 teaspoon lemon-pepper seasoning

1 teaspoon = 1 teaspoon commercial meat tenderizer (meats)

1 teaspoon = 1 teaspoon blend of parsley, marjoram, basil, lovage, dill, savory, & tarragon (salads)

1 teaspoon = 1 teaspoon blend of lovage, basil, marjoram, parsley, bay, savory & thyme (soups)

1 teaspoon = 1 teaspoon blend of pepper, garlic powder, paprika, thyme, sesame seeds, dry mustard, & savory (vegetables)

1 teaspoon = 1 teaspoon blend of sage, thyme, savory, marjoram, lovage, basil, & parsley (poultry)

1 teaspoon = 1 teaspoon blend of dill, rue, lemon balm, basil, savory, rosemary, & fennel leaves (fish)

1 teaspoon = 1 teaspoon blend of parsley, basil, lovage, marjoram, thyme, sage, & savory (beef)

1 teaspoon = 1 teaspoon blend of dry mustard, paprika, oregano, garlic powder, & onion powder (general)

22

SPICES

There are many substitutions that come close in replacing the original ingredient in dealing with spices. Then there are others that simply approximate the taste of the original. Those that approximate a taste are preceded with the symbol ``.

When you are unsure about a particular spice, it is best to mix up a small amount of the dish and test it first. Most of the time several choices are given to pick from, and you may find it necessary to test them all before you decide which ones work for you, due to the fact that any spice substitution will probably change the flavor of your dish to some degree.

FRESH HERBS

1 tablespoon = 1 teaspoon dried

DRIED LEAF HERBS

1 teaspoon = 1/4 teaspoon powdered

MIXED HERBS

1 tablespoon = 1 tablespoon thyme

ALEXANDER'S

1 tablespoon = 1/2 tablespoon parsley & 1/2 tablespoon celery flakes

ALFALFA SPROUTS

1 cup = 1 cup sunflower seed sprouts

1 cup = 1 cup lentil sprouts

ALLSPICE

1 tablespoon = 1 tablespoon blend of mace, cloves, nutmeg, & cardomom

ANISE

1 tablespoon = 1 tablespoon licorice

1 tablespoon = 1 tablespoon fennel seeds

1 tablespoon = 1 tablespoon sweet cumin

1 tablespoon = 1 tablespoon star anise

1 tablespoon = 1 tablespoon szechwan peppercorns

ARUGULA

1 tablespoon `` 1 teaspoon pepper, 1 teaspoon mustard, & 1 teaspoon peanut powder

1 tablespoon `` 1/2 tablespoon peanut powder & 1/2 tablespoon horseradish

DRIED BASIL

1 tablespoon = 1 tablespoon tarragon

1 tablespoon `` 1/2 tablespoon curry

FRESH BASIL

1 tablespoon `` 1 teaspoon cloves

LEMON BASIL

1 tablespoon `` 1/2 tablespoon lemon

LICORICE BASIL

1 tablespoon = 1/2 tablespoon licorice

SWEET BASIL

1 tablespoon `` 1/2 tablespoon anise

BAY LEAVES

1 tablespoon = 1 tablespoon tej pat

1 tablespoon = 1 tablespoon thyme

1 whole = 1/8 teaspoon ground

1 whole = 1/4 teaspoon crumbled

BITTER FLAVORS

1 tablespoon = 1 tablespoon orange
bitters

1 tablespoon = 1 tablespoon angostura
bitters

INTENSE BITTERS

1 tablespoon = 1 tablespoon dandelion

1 tablespoon = 1 tablespoon gentian
root

1 tablespoon = 1 tablespoon quinine

1 tablespoon = 1 tablespoon aloes

1 tablespoon = 1 tablespoon quassia
chips

BURNET

1 tablespoon = 1/2 cup cucumber

CARAWAY SEED

1 tablespoon `` 1 tablespoon cumin seed

1 tablespoon = 1 tablespoon caraway thyme

1 tablespoon = 1 tablespoon fennel seeds

CARAWAY LEAVES

1 tablespoon `` 1/2 tablespoon parsley & 1/2 tablespoon chervil (soups, salads)

1 tablespoon `` 1/2 tablespoon parsley & 1/2 tablespoon dill (soups, salads)

CARDOMOM

1 tablespoon ground = 1 tablespoon crushed cardamom seeds

CAPER

1 tablespoon = 1 tablespoon marsh marigold buds

1 tablespoon = 1 tablespoon pickled green nasturtium seeds

1 tablespoon = 1 tablespoon broom buds

CAYENNE PEPPER

1 tablespoon = 1 tablespoon ground hot chili pepper

1/8 teaspoon = 3-4 drops hot pepper sauce

CELERY SALT

1 tablespoon = 2 teaspoons crushed celery seed & 1 teaspoon salt

CELERY SEED

1 tablespoon = 1 tablespoon dill seed

CHILI POWDER

1 tablespoon = 1 tablespoon blend of ground chili peppers, oregano, cumin, garlic, cloves, & salt

1 tablespoon = 1 tablespoon cayenne pepper

CHERRY FLAVOR

1 pinch = 1 teaspoon grenadine syrup

CHERVIL

1 tablespoon = 1 tablespoon parsley

1 tablespoon `` 1 tablespoon anise

GARDEN CHERVIL

1 tablespoon = 1 tablespoon herb yarrow (garnish)

1 tablespoon = 1 tablespoon milfoil (garnish)

CHIVES

1 tablespoon `` 1 tablespoon chopped green onions

YELLOW CHIVES

1 tablespoon `` 1 tablespoon sweet onions

CILANTRO

1 tablespoon = 1 tablespoon celery flakes

1 tablespoon = 2 tablespoons parsley

CINNAMON

1 tablespoon = 1 tablespoon mace

1 tablespoon = 1 tablespoon cassia

1 tablespoon = 1 cinnamon stick

CINNAMON STICKS

1 stick = 1 tablespoon mace

1 stick = 1 tablespoon ground cinnamon

CLOVES

1 tablespoon = 1 tablespoon aven's root

1 tablespoon = 1 tablespoon allspice

COMFREY

1 tablespoon `` 1 tablespoon borage

1 tablespoon `` 1 tablespoon viper's bu-gloss

1 tablespoon `` 1 tablespoon anchusa

CORIANDER

1 tablespoon = 1 tablespoon cilantro

1 tablespoon = 1 tablespoon sage & 3-4 drops lemon juice

1 tablespoon = 1 tablespoon chinese parsley

CURRY POWDER

1 tablespoon = 1 tablespoon blend of ground red chili pepper, coriander, ginger, cumin, & tumeric

DILL

1 tablespoon `` 1 tablespoon caraway leaves

DILL SEED

1 tablespoon = 1 tablespoon celery seed

GINGER

1 tablespoon = 1 tablespoon greater galangal

ENDIVE

1 tablespoon = 1 tablespoon chicory

FENNEL LEAVES

1 tablespoon `` 1 tablespoon dill

SWEET FENNEL SEEDS

1 tablespoon = 1 tablespoon anise seed

1 tablespoon = 1 tablespoon licorice

GARLIC

1 clove = 1 tablespoon garlic chives

1 clove = 1 tablespoon Chinese chives

1 clove = 1/4 teaspoon minced

1 clove small = 1/4 teaspoon garlic powder

1 clove large = 1/2 teaspoon garlic powder

MILD GARLIC

1 clove = 1 tablespoon rocambole

GINGER

1 tablespoon = 1 tablespoon zedoary

1 tablespoon ground = 1 teaspoon mace & 2 teaspoons lemon peel

1/8 teaspoon ground = 1 tablespoon washed candied ginger

1/2 teaspoon fresh chopped = 1 teaspoon washed candied ginger

1 tablespoon fresh chopped = 1/4 teaspoon ground

HOPS

1 tablespoon = 1 tablespoon quassia

HOT PEPPER

1 tablespoon = 1 tablespoon Scotch bonnee pepper

1 tablespoon = 1 tablespoon bird pepper

LEMON JUICE

1 tablespoon = 1 tablespoon lemon thyme

1 tablespoon = 1 tablespoon doone valley lemon thyme

3 tablespoons = 1 lemon

1 tablespoon = 1 tablespoon sumac

1 tablespoon = 1 tablespoon sorrel

1 tablespoon = 1 tablespoon lemon grass

1 tablespoon = 1 tablespoon verbena herb

1 tablespoon = 1 tablespoon vinegar

LEMON PEEL

1 tablespoon = 1 tablespoon marma-
lade

1 tablespoon = 1/2 tablespoon dried
lime peel

1 tablespoon = 1/2 tablespoon lemon
extract

1 tablespoon = 1 tablespoon orange
peel

1 tablespoon = 1 tablespoon balm

LEMON-PEPPER SEASONING

1 tablespoon = 1 tablespoon blend of
lemon peel, salt, pepper, garlic, & onion

LENTIL SPROUTS

1 cup = 1 cup alfalfa sprouts

1 cup = 1 cup mung bean sprouts

LICORICE

1 tablespoon = 1 tablespoon Chinese 6
spice powder

1 tablespoon = 1 tablespoon anise seed

LIME JUICE

2 tablespoons = 1 lime

1 tablespoon = 1 tablespoon lemon juice

LOVAGE

1 tablespoon `` 1/2 tablespoon celery seed & 1/2 tablespoon anise seed

MACE

1 tablespoon = 1 tablespoon nutmeg

1 tablespoon = 1 tablespoon cinnamon

MARIGOLD

1 tablespoon `` 1/2 tablespoon anise & 1/2 tablespoon mint

MARJORAM

1 tablespoon = 1 tablespoon thyme

1 tablespoon `` 1 tablespoon oregano

MEAT SEASONING

1 tablespoon = 1 package onion soup mix

MEAT TENDERIZER

1/2 tablespoon = 1 cup yogurt

1/2 tablespoon = 1 cup wine

1/2 tablespoon = 2 tablespoons papaya juice (let sit a few hours)

1/2 tablespoon = 2 tablespoons lemon juice (let sit a few hours)

1/2 tablespoon = 1 tablespoon vinegar & 1 tablespoon olive oil (let sit a few hours)

MEAT FLAVOR

1 pinch = 1 tablespoon marmite yeast tenderizer

MINT

1 tablespoon = 1 tablespoon lemon balm

1 tablespoon = 1 tablespoon yerba buena

1 tablespoon = 1 tablespoon hyssop (liquors)

1 tablespoon fresh chopped = 1 tablespoon dried

MUSK

1 tablespoon = 1 tablespoon ambrette

NASTURTIUM LEAVES

1 tablespoon `` 1/2 tablespoon pepper & 1/2 tablespoon watercress

NUTMEG

1 tablespoon = 1 tablespoon cloves

1 tablespoon = 1 tablespoon mace

1 tablespoon = 1 tablespoon allspice

2 teaspoons = 1 fresh grated nutmeg

ORANGE PEEL

1 tablespoon = 1 tablespoon tangerine peel

1 tablespoon = 1 tablespoon marma-lade

1 tablespoon = 1 tablespoon mandarin orange peel

1 tablespoon = 1 tablespoon lime peel

1 tablespoon = 1/2 tablespoon orange extract

1 tablespoon fresh = 1/2 tablespoon dried

PICKLING SPICE

1 tablespoon = 1 tablespoon blend of mustard seed, dill, cinnamon, cloves, coriander, ginger, bay leaves & pepper

OREGANO

1 tablespoon = 1 tablespoon wild marjoram

1 tablespoon = 1 tablespoon oregano thyme

PAPRIKA

1 tablespoon = 1 tablespoon tumeric & a dash of cayenne pepper

1 tablespoon = 1 tablespoon ground mild sweet chili peppers

PARSLEY LEAVES

1 tablespoon `` 1 tablespoon celery leaves

1 tablespoon = 1 tablespoon chervil

1 tablespoon fresh = 1 teaspoon dried

BLACK PEPPER

1 tablespoon = 3 cracked peppercorns

1 tablespoon = 1 tablespoon grains of paradise

1 tablespoon = 1 tablespoon nigella

1 tablespoon = 1 tablespoon white pepper

RED PEPPER

1/8 teaspoon = 3-4 drops hot sauce

1/8 teaspoon = 1/8 teaspoon cayenne pepper

RED PEPPER FLAKES

1/8 teaspoon = 1/8 teaspoon fresh hot red peppers

PEPPERMINT

1/2 tablespoon peppermint = 1 tablespoon matrimony vine leaves

PINE FLAVOR

1 pinch `` 1 tablespoon rosemary

ROSEMARY

1 tablespoon = 1/2 tablespoon marjoram & 1/2 tablespoon oregano

ROSE WATER

1/2 tablespoon = 3-4 drops rose syrup essence

SAFFLOWER

1 teaspoon = 1/2 teaspoon saffron

SAFFRON

1 teaspoon = 1 tablespoon marigold petals

1 teaspoon = 1 teaspoon annatto

1 teaspoon = 1 tablespoon bijol

1 teaspoon = 1 teaspoon tumeric (color)

1 teaspoon = 1 tablespoon safflower (color)

1 teaspoon = 1 tablespoon Mexican saffron (bastard) (color)

SAGE

1 tablespoon = 1/2 tablespoon oregano

SARSAPARILLA

1 tablespoon = 1 tablespoon hoja santa

SAVORY

1 tablespoon `` 1/2 tablespoon pepper

1 tablespoon = 1 tablespoon salt

SMOKE FLAVOR

1 pinch = 1 teaspoon smoke flavored salt

1 pinch = 1 tablespoon liquid smoke

GARDEN SORREL

1 tablespoon = 1 tablespoon wood sorrel

SOY SAUCE

1 tablespoon = 1 tablespoon tamari

1 tablespoon = 1 tablespoon brewer's yeast

STAR ANISE

1 tablespoon = 1 tablespoon anise

1 tablespoon = 1 tablespoon licorice

STRAWBERRY FLAVOR

1 strawberry = 1 teaspoon strawberry extract

SUNFLOWER SEED SPROUTS

1 cup = 1 cup lentil sprouts

1 cup = 1 cup alfalfa sprouts

SWEET CICELY

1 tablespoon `` 1/2 tablespoon anise
seed & 1/2 tablespoon licorice

TARRAGON

1 tablespoon = 1 tablespoon tagetes
lucida

1 tablespoon = 2 tablespoons chervil

1 tablespoon = 2 tablespoons parsley

TARRAGON LEAVES

1 tablespoon `` 1/2 tablespoon anise &
1/2 tablespoon licorice

THYME

1 tablespoon = 1 tablespoon marjoram

1 tablespoon = 1 tablespoon satureja
thymbra savory

1 tablespoon = 1 tablespoon ajowan

1 tablespoon = 1 teaspoon marjoram, 1 teaspoon parsley, & 1 bay leaf

TUMERIC

1 tablespoon = 1 tablespoon mustard powder

WHITE PEPPER

1 teaspoon = 1 teaspoon black pepper

VANILLA EXTRACT

1 teaspoon = 1 vanilla bean

1 teaspoon = 1 teaspoon almond extract

MY OWN SUBSTITUTIONS

23

SUGAR

There are many choices in substituting for sugar.

If you want a particular flavor, you can use an extract with corn syrup which also gives you sweetness.

If it's fruit syrup you want, you can make your own by boiling down fruit puree in water.

One thing to note is that when substituting honey, corn syrup, or molasses for granulated sugar, the liquid in the recipe should be reduced by an equal amount. Also, you may need to lower the temperature to avoid browning. (See the specific substitution)

GRANULATED SUGAR

1 cup = 1 1/3 cup raw sugar

1 cup = 1/2 cup fructose sugar

1 cup = 1 cup corn syrup (reduce recipe liquid by 1/4 cup)

1 cup = 1 cup date sugar

1 cup = 1 cup packed brown sugar

1 cup = 1 1/4 cup maple sugar

1 cup = 1 cup honey & 1/2 teaspoon baking soda (reduce recipe liquid by 1/4 cup & lower temperature 25 degrees. If no liquid, add 1/4 cup flour)

1 cup = 1 cup molasses & 1/2 teaspoon baking soda (reduce recipe liquid by 1/4 cup & lower temperature 25 degrees. If no liquid, add 1/4 cup flour)

1 cup = 1 1/2 cup dissolved rock sugar

CANE SUGAR

1 cup = 1 cup solid sugar chips

POWDERED SUGAR

1 1/2 cup = 1 cup granulated sugar & 2 tablespoons cornstarch

BROWN SUGAR

1 cup = 1 cup raw sugar

1 cup = 1 cup granulated sugar & 2 tablespoons molasses

1 cup = 1 cup granulated sugar & 2 tablespoons dark corn syrup

MAPLE SUGAR

1 cup = 3/4 cup granulated sugar

HONEY

1 cup = 1 cup granulated sugar & 1/4 cup liquid

1 cup = 1 cup corn syrup

1 cup = 1 cup malt extract syrup

1 cup = 1 cup fruit syrup (boil 4 cups fruit juice to 1/4 original volume)

MAPLE SYRUP

1 cup = 1 cup fruit syrup (boil 4 cups fruit juice to 1/4 original volume)

1 cup = 1 cup honey

1 cup = 1 cup molasses

1 cup = 1 cup barley malt syrup

1 cup = 1 cup granulated sugar & 1/4 cup liquid

1 cup = 1/2 cup maple sugar & 1/2 cup liquid

CHERRY SYRUP

1 cup = 1 cup cherry puree, 1/2 cup sugar, & 2 cups water (boil down)

CORN SYRUP

1 cup = 1 cup granulated sugar & 1/4 cup liquid

1 cup = 1 cup beet sugar & 1/4 cup liquid

1 cup = 1 cup date sugar & 1/4 cup liquid

1 cup = 1 cup maple sugar & 1/4 cup liquid

1 cup = 1 cup maple syrup

GRAPE JAM

1 cup = 1 cup grape jelly

GRAPE JELLY

1 cup = 1 cup grape preserves

MARSHMELLOWS

1 cup = 1 cup bottled Marshmellow Whip

24

THICKENING AGENTS & OTHER FLOURS

There are many different thickening agents that you can use in cooking, and it is likely that one or more of them will be in your baking cabinet.

If it's gravy you want to thicken, you can use ground nuts, seeds, beans, or even plain gelatin.

If it's soup you want to thicken, you can use peanut butter, dried vegetables, or mashed potatoes.

There are starches, meals, and flours of many varieties listed that can all do a good job for you.

ARROWROOT

1 teaspoon = 1 tablespoon white flour

1 teaspoon = 1/2 tablespoon cornstarch

CORNSTARCH

1 tablespoon = 2 tablespoons arrowroot

1 tablespoon = 1 tablespoon ricestarch

1 tablespoon = 2 tablespoons quick cooking tapioca

1 tablespoon = 1 tablespoon water chestnut flour

FINE CORNMEAL

1 tablespoon = 1 tablespoon coarse cornmeal

CORNMEAL

1 tablespoon = 1 tablespoon millet grit

1 tablespoon = 1 tablespoon sesame meal

1 tablespoon = 1 tablespoon soy grit

1 cup = 1 cup white flour (coatings)

FARINA

1 tablespoon = 1 tablespoon semolina coarse ground flour

GARBANZO BEAN FLOUR

2 tablespoons = 1/2 tablespoon white flour

OATMEAL

1 tablespoon = 1 tablespoon fine rolled oats

1 tablespoon = 1 tablespoon millet

POTATO FLOUR

1 tablespoon = 1 tablespoon cornstarch

1 tablespoon = 1 tablespoon rice flour

1 tablespoon = 2 tablespoons white flour

POTATO STARCH

1 tablespoon = 1 tablespoon cornstarch

1 tablespoon = 1 tablespoon lotus root starch

1 tablespoon = 1 tablespoon ricestarch

1 tablespoon = 1 tablespoon tapioca flour

RICE FLOUR

1 tablespoon = 1 tablespoon quick cooking tapioca flour

1 tablespoon = 1 tablespoon rice flakes

1 tablespoon = 1 tablespoon soy flour

SEMOLINA GRAIN MEAL

1 cup = 1 cup cooked rice

1 tablespoon = 1 tablespoon wheat farina

1 cup = 1 cup cream of wheat

SOY FLOUR

1 tablespoon = 1 tablespoon oat flour

1 tablespoon = 1 tablespoon wheat flour

1 tablespoon = 1 tablespoon chick-pea flour

WHOLE WHEAT FLOUR

1 cup = 2/3 cup white flour & 1/3 cup bran

1 cup = 2/3 cup white flour & 1/3 cup wheat germ

1 cup = 1 cup graham flour

ANY FLOUR

1 tablespoon = 1 egg (gravy)

1 tablespoon = 1/2 tablespoon gelatin (gravy)

1 tablespoon = 1 teaspoon xanthan gum (gravy)

1 tablespoon = 1 tablespoon ground nut flour

1 tablespoon = 1 tablespoon ground seed flour

1 tablespoon = 1 tablespoon bean flour

SOUP THICKENER

= 1/2 cup instant rice

= 2 tablespoons peanut butter

= 1/2 cup mashed potatoes

= 1/2 cup dried ground zucchini

= 1/2 cup dried ground squash

= 1/2 cup dried ground yams

= 1/2 cup dried ground potatoes

= 1/2 cup dried ground eggplant

= 1/2 cup dried ground pumpkin

= 1/2 cup dried ground carrots

MY OWN SUBSTITUTIONS

25

VEGETABLES

Vegetables are hard to substitute for because each one tastes so unique.

However, there are alot of close substitutions to be found. For instance, pimento tastes an awful lot like sweet red bell peppers. And leeks substitute for green onions very well.

You can use baby butter beans for garbanzo beans or radish sprouts for bean sprouts.

Shallots can replace onions and garlic for you at the same time, as they taste halfway in between.

ARTICHOKES

1 cup = 1 cup cardoons

1 cup = 1 cup lotus root

1 cup = 1 cup cooked kohlrabi

AVACADOES

2 seasoned = 1 can avacado dip

BABY BUTTER BEANS

1 cup = 1 cup garbanzo beans

BUTTER BEANS

1 cup = 1 cup lima beans

FRENCH GREEN BEANS

1 cup = 1 cup winged beans

GARBANZO BEANS

1 cup = 1 cup baby butter beans

1 cup = 1 cup lima beans

WHOLE GREEN BEANS

1 cup = 1 cup French style green beans

1 cup = 1 cup yellow beans

LIMA BEANS

1 cup = 1 cup fava beans

1 cup = 1 cup butter beans

BABY LIMA BEANS

1 cup = 1 cup navy beans

MUNG BEANS

1 cup = 1 cup split peas

NAVY BEANS

1 cup = 1 cup great northern beans

1 cup = 1 cup baby white lima beans

1 cup = 1 cup black-eyed peas

PINTO BEANS

1 cup = 1 cup red kidney beans

RED KIDNEY BEANS

1 cup = 1 cup pink beans

1 cup = 1 cup pinto beans

SOYBEANS

1 cup = 1 cup lima beans

BEAN SPROUTS

1 cup = 1 cup radish sprouts

1 cup = 1 cup mung bean sprouts

1 cup = 1 cup alfalfa sprouts

1 cup = 1 cup celery

MUNG BEAN SPROUTS

1 cup `` 1/2 cup peanuts & 1/2 cup celery

SWEET BELL PEPPER

1 pepper = 1 Italian pepper

1 pepper = 1 Hungarian wax pepper

SWEET RED PEPPER

1 pepper = 2 tablespoon pimento

SWEET YELLOW BELL PEPPER

1 pepper = 1 green bell pepper

SWEET ORANGE BELL PEPPER

1 pepper = 1 green bell pepper

GREEN BELL PEPPER

2 tablespoons diced = 1 tablespoon dry

1 pepper = 1 sweet purple-brown bell pepper

1 pepper = 1 sweet yellow bell pepper

1 pepper = 1 sweet orange bell pepper

BROCCOLI

1 cup chopped = 1 cup chopped Chinese broccoli

GREEN CABBAGE

1 cup chopped = 1 cup kohlrabi

1 cup chopped = 1 cup red cabbage

BOK CHOY CELERY CABBAGE

1 cup = 1 cup bok choy sum cabbage

RED CABBAGE

1 cup chopped = 1 cup green cabbage

NAPA CABBAGE

1 cup `` 1/2 cup celery & 1/2 cup cabbage

SWAMP CABBAGE

1 cup = 1 cup canned hearts of palm

CARROTS

1 cup = 1 cup white turnips

1 cup = 1 cup parsnips

CAULIFLOWER

1 cup cut = 1 cup cut kohlrabi

CELERY

1 cup chopped = 1 cup Chinese celery

1 cup chopped = 1 cup fennel

1 cup chopped = 1 cup celeriac

1 cup chopped = 1 cup Belgian endive

CHICORY

1 cup chopped = 1 cup spinach

COLLARDS

1 cup chopped = 1 cup mild cabbage

YELLOW CORN

1 cup = 1 cup yellow squash (with seeds)

CUCUMBER

1/2 cup sliced = 2 tablespoons borage leaves

1/2 cup sliced = 2 tablespoons salad burnet

1/2 cup sliced = 2 tablespoons viper's bugloss

DAIKON

1 cup sliced = 1 cup radishes

DILL PICKLES

1 pickle = 1 sliced sweet pickle in dill water

CURLY ENDIVE

1 cup = 1 cup chicory

1 cup = 1 cup escarole

BELGIUM ENDIVE

1 cup chopped = 1 cup radicchio

1 cup chopped = 1 cup fennel

ESCAROLE

1 cup chopped = 1 cup chicory

1 cup chopped = 1 cup arugula

FIDDLEHEADS

　　1 cup `` 1/2 cup asparagus & 1/2 cup green snap beans

GOURD

　　1 gourd = 1 winter melon

KALE

　　1 cup chopped = 1 cup spinach

KOHLRABI

　　1 cup chopped = 1 cup celeriac

　　1 cup chopped = 1 cup radishes

LEEKS

　　1 cup chopped = 1 cup green onions

HEAD LETTUCE

　　1 head = 1 stalk green leaf lettuce

　　1 head = 1 stalk romaine lettuce

MUSTARD GREENS

　　1 cup chopped = 1 cup Chinese mustard cabbage

OKRA

1 cup fresh = 1 eggplant

ONIONS

1 cup chopped = 1 cup shallots (do not sautee to avoid bitterness)

1/2 cup chopped = 1 package onion soup mix

1/4 cup fresh = 1 tablespoon dry minced

1/4 cup fresh = 1 teaspoon onion powder

1/4 cup fresh = 1 teaspoon onion salt

WHITE ONIONS

1 cup chopped = 1 cup yellow onions

SWEET ONIONS

1 cup chopped = 1 cup leeks

1 cup = 1 cup sauteed white onions

MINCED ONIONS

1 tablespoon = 1 tablespoon chives

PARSNIPS

1 cup = 1 cup carrots

1 cup = 1 cup white turnips

1 cup = 1 cup parsley root

GARDEN PEAS

1 cup = 1 cup pigeon peas

SPLIT PEAS

1 cup = 1 cup sweet peas

1 cup = 1 cup mung beans

SWEET PEAS

1 cup = 1 cup pea shoots

1 cup = 1 cup split peas

SNOW PEAS

1 cup = 1 cup sugar snap peas

PIMENTO

2 tablespoons = 1/2 cup sweet red bell pepper

POTATOES

1 cup sliced = 1 cup taro root

1 cup sliced = 1 cup frozen hash browns

1 cup sliced = 1 cup frozen french fries

WHITE IRISH POTATOES

1 cup = 1 cup small white turnips

1 cup = 1 cup sweet cassava

1 cup = 1 cup boniato

1 cup = 1 cup tannia

FRENCH FRIED POTATOES

1 cup = 1 cup tator tots

1 cup = 1 cup frozen hash browns

TATOR TOT POTATOES

1 cup = 1 cup frozen hash browns

HASH BROWN POTATOES

1 cup = 1 cup french fries

PUMPKIN

1 cup = 1 cup acorn squash

1 cup = 1 cup butternut squash

1 cup = 1 cup yellow winter squash

RADISH SPROUTS

1 cup = 1 cup mustard cress

RED RADISHES

1 cup = 1 cup daikon

1 cup = 1 cup black radishes

1 cup = 1 cup white icicle radishes

SHALLOTS

1 cup chopped = 7/8 cup chopped onion
& 1/8 cup chopped garlic

SPAGHETTI SQUASH

1 cup = 1 cup pasta

SPINACH

1 cup chopped = 1 cup escarole

1 cup chopped = 1 cup kale

1 cup chopped = 1 cup callaloo

1 cup chopped = 1 cup sorrel

1 cup chopped = 1 cup swiss chard

1 cup chopped = 1 cup cut amaranth

YELLOW SQUASH

1 squash = 1 calabaza

BUTTERNUT SQUASH

1 squash = 1 hubbard squash

1 squash = 1 acorn squash

ACORN SQUASH

1 squash = 1 banana squash

SWEET POTATO

1 potato = 1 yam

TOMATOES

2 cup fresh = 1 can stewed (soups)

1 cup fresh = 3/4 cup water & 1/4 cup tomato replacer (cooking)

TURNIPS

1 cup chopped = 1 cup jicama

1 cup chopped = 1 cup rutabagas

1 cup chopped = 1 cup carrots

WATER CHESTNUTS

1 cup = 1 cup American cress

WATERCRESS

1 cup = 1 cup mustard cress

1 cup = 1 cup sunflower sprouts

1 cup = 1 cup yellow rocket

1 cup = 1 cup lady's smock

1 cup = 1 cup alfalfa sprouts

WHITE TURNIPS

1 cup = 1 cup parsnips

GREEN ZUCCHINI

1 cup = 1 cup yellow zucchini

1 cup = 1 cup angled luffa

1 cup = 1 cup yellow squash

1 cup = 1 cup pattypan squash

YAM

1 yam = 1 sweet potato

26

WHITE FLOUR

Wheatier flours, when used as substitutions for white flour, will get brown sooner, so they should be watched, and some oil may need to be replaced with water for the same reason. (See the specific substitution)

It should be noted that using different flours will change the taste of your baked goods to some degree. Some more than others. Using wheatier flours will make your food taste wheatier. But using peanut or sunflower seed flours will make your food taste nutty.

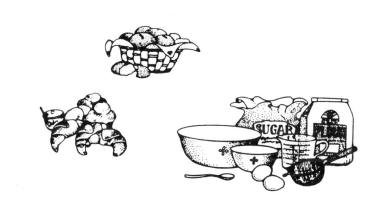

WHITE FLOUR

1 cup = 1 cup amaranth flour

2 cups = 1 cup arrowroot

1 cup = 1 cup barley flour

1 tablespoon = 1 tablespoon bean flour (gravy)

1 cup = 1 cup brown rice flour

1 cup = 1 cup buckwheat flour

1 cup - 2 tablespoons = 1 cup cake flour

1 cup = 1 cup corn flour

1 cup = 1 cup fine cornmeal (coatings)

2 cups = 1 cup cornstarch

1 cup = 1 cup millet flour

1 tablespoon = 1 tablespoon nut flour (gravy)

1 cup = 1 cup oat flour

1 tablespoon = 1 1/2 tablespoons peanut butter (soups)

1 cup = 1 cup peanut flour

2 cups = 1 cup potato flour

1 cup = 1/2 cup potato starch

1 cup = 1/2 cup rice flour

1 cup = 1 1/3 cup rye flour (replace 1 tablespoon oil with 1 tablespoon water)

1 cup = 1 cup soy flour

1 cup = 1 cup sunflower seed meal

1 cup = 1 cup tapioca flour

1 tablespoon = 2 teaspoons quick cooking tapioca

1 cup = 7/8 cup whole wheat flour (replace 1 tablepoon oil with 1 tablespoon water)

1 cup = 3/4 cup whole wheat flour & 1/4 cup wheat germ (replace 1 tablespoon oil with 1 tablespoon water)

CAKE FLOUR

1 cup = 1 cup - 2 tablespoons white flour & 2 tablespoons corn starch

SELF-RISING FLOUR

1 cup = 1 cup all-purpose flour, 1 1/2 teaspoons baking powder, & 1/8 teaspoon salt

SIFTED WHITE FLOUR

1 cup = 1 cup - 2 tablespoons unsifted white flour

27

WINE & LIQUORS

Extracts, such as brandy extract, can be used for flavor. Fruit flavored liqueors can be used when certain flavors like orange, apricot, or cherry are desired.

The alcohol content will evaporate when heated, so wines and spirits are good meat tenderizers.

If sweetness is desired, wines like Sherry or Port are usually used. Otherwise drier wines are better to cook with.

If you wish to remove the alcoholic content, there are some non-alcoholic substitutions presented also.

ANISEED FLAVOR
   = Anis

   = Anisette

   = Pastis

   = Ouzo

CARAWAY FLAVOR

   = Kummel

CUMIN FLAVOR

   = Kummel

FRUIT FLAVOR

   = fruit flavored liquors

ORANGE FLAVOR

   = Curacao

   = Grand Marnier

APRICOT FLAVOR

   = apricot flavored liquor

CHERRY FLAVOR

   = cherry flavored liquor

PEPPERMINT FLAVOR

    = Creme de Menthe

RASPBERRY FLAVOR

    = Chambord

    = Cassis

BOURBON

    = Whiskey

FRUIT BRANDY

    = Quetsch

    = Mirabelle

BRANDY

    = Imitation brandy extract

    = Rum

    = Cognac

    = Marc

BURGUNDY

    = Gamay

    = Bordeaux

CALVADOS

= Apple Cider

CHABLIS

= Chardonnay

CHAMPAYNE

= Ginger Ale

= Sparkling Wine

COGNAC

= Brandy

MADEIRA

= Cream Sherry

= Port

MARSALA

= Dry Sherry

PORT

= Cream Sherry

= Madeira

RUBY CABERNET

= Cabernet Sauvignon

SHERRY

= Madeira

= Marsala

SWEET WINE

= Madeira

= Marsala

= Framboise

RICE WINE

= Dry sherry

WHITE WINE

= Ginger Ale

= Dry Vermouth

WHITE WINE VINEGAR

= White Cider Vinegar

= Dry Vermouth

WINE

= wine coolers

RED WINE VINEGAR

= tarragon wine vinegar

RUM

= Brandy (candies)

BEER

= Bitter Hops

= alcohol-free beer

GREEK OUZO

= Whiskey

WHISKEY

= Bourbon

= American Apple Jack

= Calvados

= Turkish Raki

VODKA

= Whiskey (for flaming)

"COOKING EQUIVALENTS & MEASUREMENTS (including metric)" is another book by the author created to supplement the main text "1000 Cooking Substitutions". It lists over 350 equivalent measurements in cooking, such as 1 cup of dry rice is equal to 3 cups of cooked rice, or 1 cup of shredded Romano cheese is equal to 1 3 oz. package, etc. It covers fruits and vegetables, dairy, sugar, meat, and even yeast. This guide assists in less wasteful and more tasteful food preparation. It also provides for the accurate measurement of ingredients as it lists the equivalent measurements in teaspoons, tablespoons, cups, fluid oz., and pints on up, for those times when you are not sure. It gives the metric measurements as well. This handy guide is available in the library system, or it can be purchased from the publisher for $2.98. See the coupon and order form at the back of the book.

The following books were used as references in making this book, along with others too numerous to mention, spanning the entire metropolitan library system, and private collections as well.

Nancy Albright, "THE RODALE COOKBOOK", (Rodale Press, 1973)

Meredith, "THE BETTER HOMES & GARDENS COOKBOOK", (Better Homes & Gardens, 1985)

Ying, Editor, "THE NEW GOODHOUSEKEEPING COOKBOOK", (William Morrow, 1986)

Sam Gilbertie, "KITCHEN HERBS", (Bantam Books, 1988)

Jean Anderson & Elaine Hanna, "THE NEW DOUBLEDAY COOKBOOK" (Doubleday, 75)

Lucinda Hutson, "THE HERB GARDEN COOKBOOK", (Texas Monthly Press, 1987)

J. Gormans, "THE VEGETABLE COOKBOOK", (Yankee Books, 1986)

Rudolf-August Oetker, "THE BEST OF COLD FOODS", (H P Books, 1982)

Lucille Recht Tenner, "THE HONEY BOOK", (Hastings House, 1980)

Barbara Block "IT DOESN'T PAN OUT", (Dembner Books, 1981)

Nikki & David Goldbeck, "THE SUPERMARKET Handbook", (Harper & Row, 1973)

James Beard & Sam Aaron, "HOW TO EAT BETTER FOR LESS", (Simon & Shuster, 1970)

Meredith McCarty, "AMERICAN MACROBIOTIC CUISINE", (Turning Point Publications, 1986)

Patricia Galbresith, "TIPTOEING THROUGH THE KITCHEN", (Sunshine Publications, 1986)

Carl Franz & Lorena Havens, "THE ON & OFF THE ROAD COOKBOOK", (John Muir Publications, 1982)

Esther Shank, "MENNONITE COUNTRY STYLE RECIPES", (Herald Press, 1987)

American Dietetic Association, "AMERICAN DIETETIC ASSOCIATION FAMILY COOKBOOK-Volume II", (Prentice-Hall, 1984)

American Heart Association, "AMERICAN HEART ASSOCIATION COOKBOOK", (David McKay Co., Inc., 1984)

Weight Watchers, International, "WEIGHT WATCHERS FAVORITE RECIPES", (New American Library, 1986)

Carol Ann Rinzler, "THE COMPLETE BOOK OF FOOD" (World Almanac, 1987)

Conde' Nast Bks,   "THE BEST OF GOURMET" (Conde' Nast Books, 1986)

MY OWN SUBSTITUTIONS

NEW SUBSTITUTION COLLECTION

We continually collect new substitutions not previously printed so that we can offer the best possible book. In doing so, we can expand the choices available for the largest number of ingredients, and bring to the public all known choices of value to date.

This collection is continually revised and updated. It will be included in the next edition of "1000 Cooking Substitutions", and currently can be added to existing books as an appendix.

If you do not want to wait for the next edition of "1000 Cooking Substitutions", this collection can be purchased <u>directly</u> from Global Trade Co., Inc., P.O. Box 571, Dept B, Bethany, OK 73008 for $5.00.

REFERRALS

If you have a friend or friends that you tell about this book, and they subsequently order a copy, we will send you a free copy of "Cooking Equivalents & Measurements", or a $3.00 check, whichever you prefer. There are no limits to the number of referrals you may have.

Your friend or friends can also take advantage of the special coupon offer at the back of the book. Simply photocopy the coupon page, fill it out for them, and hand it to them to send in. In this way you will be assured of receiving proper credit, and your friends will receive a discount as well. Also, be sure to indicate which gift you prefer by circling (M) for money or (B) for book right next to your name.

Ordering information is given at the back of the book.

Bookstores are ineligible for this offer.

MAKE EXTRA CASH

"1000 Cooking Substitutions" is currently experiencing tremendous success. An unusually high 90% of the people recently polled expressed a desire to own this book.

Every kitchen needs this book. It is the only reference book available on this subject at this time, and as such is in great demand.

It offers great opportunity to anyone who would like to make extra money selling it. If you would like to participate, all you need to do is to tell everyone you know about it. When they place an order, you will automatically receive a check for $3.00 each and every time.

Word of mouth sales has proven to be our greatest success. Write for more details, and a sales kit will be sent to you via first class mail.

Bookstores are ineligible for this offer.

SUBSTITUTION CLUB

If you know of an excellent substitution not already listed in this guide, send it to us and we will put your name in our new edition in the "Substitution Club Appendix", and feature it in the book.

SUBSTITUTE: _____

_____
_____
_____
_____
_____
_____
_____
_____
_____
_____
_____
_____
_____

NAME: _____

ADDRESS: _____

STATE & ZIP: _____

CONTEST

Once a year, on 12-15, Global Trade Co. sponsors a contest for the best substitution sent in to the Substitution Club for the year. The winner will have an exposé written up about her/him and published in "LATEST COOKBOOK NEWS", a national newsletter that is distributed across the country.

If you would like to enter your substitution, please check here:

( )

COUPON

This coupon is good for:

CHECK
ONE:

◯ **ONE FREE BOOK** ("Cooking Equivalents
& Measurements-including metric")

◯ OR **$3.00 OFF** (the regular price of
"1000 Cooking Substitutions")

when you order either the hardcover or
softcover edition of "1000 Cooking
Substitutions <u>directly</u> from Global Trade Co.,
P.O. Box 571, Dept A, Bethany, OK 73008

I was referred by: (M) (B)_____
Address:_____
State & Zip:_____
Date of his/her original purchase:_____
Location of his/her purchase:_____

ONE COUPON PER CUSTOMER

NOT VALID WITH ANY OTHER OFFER

This coupon may expire without prior notice

ORDER FORM

All books unconditionally guaranteed when returned within 15 days.

Please send me the following books:

QUANTITY	TITLE OF BOOK	PRICE
	(Softcover) "1000 Cooking Substitutions"	15.95
	(Hardcover) "1000 Cooking Substitutions"	22.95
	"New Substitution Collection"	5.00
	"Cooking Equivalents & Measurements-incl. metric"	2.98

SUBTOTAL:_____
POSTAGE & PACKAGING:_____
(First book $1.50, each additional one add .50)
(OK residents ONLY add 6% sales tax) **SALES TAX:**_____
COUPON CREDIT, if applicable:_____
TOTAL ENCLOSED:_____

ORDER NOW

Your name:_____
Address:_____
State & Zip:_____

Mail your check or money order to: **THANK**
Global Trade Co., Inc. **YOU**
P.O. Box 571, Dept A **FOR**
Bethany, OK 73008 **YOUR**
ORDER!

Money orders please allow 2-3 weeks.
Checks please allow approximately 4 wks.